THE LIGHT WITHIN

An Invitation to Inner Stillness and Grace

By Fuchen Yew

ISBN: 978-1-61611-299-8

This book is a work of personal reflection. It is not affiliated with, nor representative of, any religious or institutional teaching. The content is offered solely as an invitation to inner inquiry, presence, and peace.

Paperback First Edition — July 2025

www.JoytitudeAcademy.com

This Book is for:

May these words meet you gently,
and remind you of the quiet light
that has always lived within.

From the Author

This book was not planned — it arrived.
In quiet mornings and long walks.
In the stillness after storms.
In the gentle ache of remembering what truly matters.

Each word emerged like a lantern in the dark,
asking only to be noticed.
To be listened to.
To be lived.

I wrote *The Light Within* not because I had answers,
but because something in me longed to share what had
been quietly gathered.
Not to teach, but to reflect.
Not to explain, but to offer.

If this little book has found you,
I trust it was meant to.
Let it be what it needs to be:
a companion,
a mirror,
a breath.

— Fuchen Yew

Dedication

To my parents, whose quiet love has been a steady light in my life, not through grand words, but through the gentle grace of their everyday care.

And to Pastor Hunker, who opened his heart to a stranger with kindness and warmth, showing me, in a simple act of welcome, the boundless reach of compassion.

"I wish I could show you when you are lonely or in darkness the astonishing light of your own being."

— Hafiz

Preface: A Journey Remembered

For many years, I have felt a quiet call to write a spiritual book — not to teach, but to share. Not to explain, but to reflect. Something in me knew that the experiences, insights, and inner shifts I had gathered over the years were not meant to stay hidden. They were meant to be offered — gently, honestly, in service of those walking their own path of awakening.

I studied engineering in the United States and began my career in the North American telecommunications industry — a world shaped by structure, logic, and precision. It gave me tools to build and solve, to measure and organize. But in time, I began to sense that it wasn't the whole story.

When I returned to Malaysia in 2005, my life quietly began to shift. Encounters with spiritual teachers, and moments of deep inner questioning, opened me to another way of learning — one rooted not in data, but in presence; not in analysis, but in awareness.

Since then, I've devoted myself to spiritual study and practice — not in a formal or institutional sense, but as a way of life. Along this journey, I've learned that the deepest truths are often the simplest. And that the light we seek is not somewhere else — it's already within us, waiting to be remembered.

This book is my offering — a reflection of what I've gathered along the way, and a quiet companion for those seeking peace, clarity, and truth in their own lives.

Take your time with it. Let the words settle. May you feel understood, perhaps even gently held. And more than anything, I hope it reminds you that the light you're looking for has always lived within you.

With love and gratitude,
Fuchen Yew
Malaysia, July 2025

Table of Contents

Introduction: An Invitation to the Heart

There comes a time in every soul's life when the outer world no longer satisfies the inner thirst. We begin to sense that beyond our daily routines, our striving, our relationships, and even our pain — there is something deeper calling us. Not louder, but quieter. Not demanding, but ever-present. This book is a response to that call.

It is not tied to any religion or doctrine. You don't need to believe in any particular tradition, teacher, or system. What you will find here are timeless spiritual principles — compassion, forgiveness, surrender, stillness, love — offered with humility and simplicity. These teachings are meant to speak not to your intellect, but to your soul.

You may be carrying burdens you can't name. Or seeking peace you've never quite found. Or simply ready to live with greater clarity, strength, and meaning. Whatever brings you here, welcome. This book is a companion for the inward journey — a path not toward perfection, but toward presence.

Throughout these pages, you'll find spiritual reflections drawn from deep wells of insight and inner inquiry. Some may feel like familiar truths you had forgotten. Others may gently challenge your habits of thought and perception. Each chapter offers not just understanding, but an invitation — to turn inward, to soften, to awaken.

You do not need to strive to "get it right." The truths shared here already live inside you. You have always known how to love, how to forgive, how to be still. This book is here to help you remember.

It is written with reverence for the unseen and the sacred. With compassion for every human struggle. And with faith — not in any single belief, but in the intelligence of life itself, which guides us back to the heart when we are ready.

This is not a path of escape. It is a path of embodiment. To walk in the world with grace. To love without needing anything in return. To let go of what was, and trust what is.

So take your time. Read slowly. Let your heart listen as much as your mind.

This is the beginning of a return — not to somewhere new, but to who you've always been.

Contemplation

What is stirring in my heart as I begin this book?

What am I seeking—not in the future, but right now?

Can I allow myself to be exactly where I am, with kindness?

Gentle Practice

Close your eyes for a moment. Place a hand on your heart. Take three slow breaths, feeling your chest rise and fall. Whisper inwardly: *I am here. I am open. I am enough.* Let this be your first step—a quiet return to yourself.

Part I: THE WAY WITHIN

Chapter 1: The Power of Compassion

Compassion is not an emotion. It is not sympathy, and it is not pity. True compassion is a presence — a force of the heart that sees beyond appearances, judgments, and fear. It is the quiet knowing that every being is doing the best they can with the pain they carry and the light they have.

In the world we live in, compassion is often misunderstood as softness or weakness. But in truth, compassion is strength — not the kind that conquers, but the kind that holds, endures, and uplifts. It is the power to remain open in a world that often hardens us. It is the courage to feel deeply in a culture that tells us to numb.

Compassion doesn't always arrive as a grand gesture. Sometimes, it reveals itself in the smallest of moments — in the space between people, in the way we choose to respond to someone else's tension. I witnessed this one afternoon during a lunch break in Malaysia, in the middle of a busy coffee shop.

A young staff member at the counter, flustered by a long queue and the noise of the midday rush, had just knocked over a drink while handing it to a customer. The cup hit the counter, spilled everywhere, and for a moment, she froze — her shoulders tense, her expression uncertain.

You could almost feel the panic rise in her as she stood there, unsure what to do next.

Then, something shifted. The customer — an office worker clearly in a rush — looked at her, smiled gently, and said, "It's okay, take your time." Just six simple words, offered without frustration. That kindness seemed to ripple outward. Others in line, who had every reason to be impatient, softened. No one complained. No one sighed or scolded. They just waited — quietly, kindly.

No one sought thanks. Their presence alone was the gift.

In that small, almost unnoticeable moment, I saw how compassion isn't just about being nice. It's a force that disarms fear. A presence that calms tension. A choice that changes the energy of a room — and the weight in someone's heart.

To live with compassion is to allow the heart to lead. It is not always easy. Sometimes, the heart breaks open. Sometimes it feels easier to turn away — from suffering, from injustice, even from our own inner wounds. But when we stay, when we breathe through the discomfort and choose love anyway, we discover that compassion is a path to freedom.

Because compassion is not just for others. It begins with the self.

Many of us carry a silent cruelty toward ourselves — a voice that judges, criticizes, and withholds love. We tell ourselves we are not enough, that we should be further along, stronger, more perfect. But healing begins when we meet ourselves with kindness. When we look inward with the same tenderness we would offer a child or a dear friend.

You cannot give what you have not given to yourself.

When you learn to sit with your own pain — without shame, without resistance — you become someone who can sit with the pain of the world. You become safe. You become real. And from that place, your presence becomes a medicine.

Compassion doesn't mean rescuing others or fixing everything. It simply means being willing to see. To witness someone in their wholeness, not in their brokenness. To honor the dignity of their path, even when it is messy or unfamiliar. It means showing up — with your presence, your attention, your heart — without needing to control the outcome.

In compassion, there is no superiority. No judgment. No division. Only recognition.

Recognition that at our core, we are all the same.

We all long to be loved. We all want to feel safe. We all carry hidden stories and silent hopes. And when we begin to live from this recognition, something changes. The space between "you" and "me" softens. We begin to move through the world as though every being is part of us — because in truth, they are.

This is the power of compassion.

It melts the illusion of separation. It brings us back to the truth of our interconnectedness. It reminds us that love is not just something we feel — it is something we are.

Contemplation

Where in my life can I soften?

Where am I withholding love — from myself, or from others?

Can I sit with pain — mine or another's — without trying to fix or flee?

Gentle Practice

Today, choose to offer one silent blessing to someone who crosses your path — whether stranger or friend.

Let your heart say inwardly:

"May you be safe.

May you be free.

May you know you are loved."

You don't need to speak it aloud. Your presence carries the blessing.

Chapter 2: Letting Go Into Love

Love is not something we chase. It is not something we earn. Love is what remains when we release everything that is not love — fear, control, resentment, expectation. Love is our natural state, but we forget. We guard our hearts. We hold our breath. We cling to certainty. We try to protect ourselves from being hurt, not realizing that in the process, we shut love out.

Letting go into love means learning how to open again.

It is a surrender, not of your power, but of your resistance. It is the quiet, brave act of releasing the stories you've told yourself — about who you must be, what others must give, and how life should unfold. It is choosing to trust what you cannot yet see.

Letting go is not giving up. It is giving over. It is turning your burdens — the weight you've carried for too long — into offerings. It is saying: *I no longer need to carry this alone.*

When we let go, we create space — space for love to enter, space for healing to begin, space for grace to move in ways the mind could never plan. But to let go, we must be willing to feel. We must be willing to meet the places inside us that are clenched, guarded, afraid.

Letting go is not a one-time act. It is a practice. A rhythm. A dance. We loosen our grip. We breathe. We soften. And then, when fear comes knocking again — we breathe again. We choose again.

The deeper truth is this: you are not losing anything by letting go. You are returning to something. You are coming home.

When we hold tightly to pain, to people, to outcomes, we live in a constant state of tension. Our hearts can't breathe. But when we release — not with bitterness, but with faith — we invite life to carry us. And it always will. Life never stops flowing. It only waits for us to step into the current.

To let go is to remember that love does not need to be grasped. It only needs to be allowed.

And so we release the past, not because it didn't matter, but because it has served its purpose. We release expectations, not because we stop caring, but because we trust that something wiser is unfolding. We release the need to be understood, to be right, to be perfect — because love is more important than all of that.

Love is not a reward. It is a way of being. And it begins with this moment. This breath. This gentle letting go.

Contemplation

What am I holding onto that is no longer serving me?

What would it feel like to trust life, even just a little more?

Can I soften my grip — and allow love to hold me?

Gentle Practice

Place your hand over your heart and say silently or aloud:

"I am safe to let go.

I am held by something greater.

I surrender what no longer belongs to me. I open to love."

Then exhale slowly. Feel the release. Even a small opening is enough.

Chapter 3: Stillness Is the Path

We live in a world that celebrates speed. We are taught that movement means progress, that doing more means being more, and that stillness is wasted time.

But the truth is, some of the most profound awakenings happen in silence. Some of the deepest healings occur not when we push forward, but when we stop — and listen.

Stillness is not the absence of life. It is the presence of life, fully felt. It is where truth becomes audible, where clarity begins to rise from beneath the noise.

In stillness, the soul speaks.

The mind may resist stillness. It is used to movement, used to distractions, used to filling every space with thought. But the heart longs for silence. It knows that real peace cannot be found in doing — only in being.

When we are still, we begin to sense something greater moving through us. We remember that we are not the voice in our heads. We are the awareness beneath the voice. And from that awareness, wisdom emerges — not forced, but revealed.

Stillness is where love takes root. It is where fear dissolves, not through effort, but through gentle presence. In the quiet, we come face to face with ourselves — not our roles, not our stories, but our essence. And what we find there is not empty. It is whole.

To walk the spiritual path is to develop a relationship with stillness. Not as a rare state reserved for retreat or ritual, but as a living presence within daily life. Moments of stillness can be found in the space between breaths, in the pause before responding, in the quiet watching of a sunrise, or the way light moves through trees.

You don't have to escape the world to find silence. You simply have to turn inward.

Stillness does not mean inaction. It means conscious action. It means moving from a place of clarity rather than chaos. Speaking from truth rather than reaction. Living with awareness rather than habit.

There is a guidance available to you at all times — not loud or demanding, but steady and wise. To access it, you must become still enough to hear it. And once you hear it, trust it.

Stillness is not a luxury.

It is the path.

Contemplation

What would I hear if I slowed down long enough to listen?

Where in my life am I being invited to pause?

Am I willing to trust the wisdom that arises in silence?

Gentle Practice

Close your eyes for a few minutes. Breathe gently. Let your thoughts come and go without following them.

With each breath, say inwardly:

"I am still. I am here. I am enough."

Let yourself rest in that space — even just for a moment.

Chapter 4: The Healing Force of Forgiveness

Forgiveness is not something we do for others. It is something we do to free ourselves.

Many of us carry wounds — invisible to the world, but heavy in the heart. We replay the betrayals, the injustices, the words that should never have been spoken. We cling to the pain as if holding on will protect us, or prove that what happened mattered. And it did matter. But holding on does not heal us. Only love can do that. And forgiveness is love in action.

Forgiveness does not mean forgetting. It does not mean pretending something didn't hurt. It does not excuse the harm or erase the past. Rather, it is a conscious choice to no longer let the past define the present. It is choosing to release the chains we've wrapped around our own hearts.

When we do not forgive, we carry the weight of resentment — and resentment hardens the soul. It closes the heart, narrows the breath, poisons the mind. We think we are protecting ourselves, but in truth, we are prolonging our suffering.

To forgive is to reclaim your peace.

Sometimes the one we must forgive is someone else. Sometimes, it is ourselves. And often, it is both. The harshest judgments we carry are often directed inward. We hold onto shame, guilt, regret — punishing ourselves over and over again for what we didn't know, for who we used to be.

But what if you could meet yourself with compassion instead? What if you could see your younger self, your past self, as someone who was doing their best in the only way they knew how? What if you could recognize that healing is not linear, and that growth often comes through the very mistakes we struggle to forgive?

Forgiveness is not a destination. It is a process. A practice. Sometimes, you forgive and feel a lightness immediately. Other times, the same wound rises again — and again, you forgive. Each time, you soften. Each time, you reclaim another piece of your power.

There is no weakness in forgiveness. There is only strength, and liberation.

You don't forgive because someone deserves it. You forgive because you deserve peace.

Letting go of blame does not make you smaller. It makes you whole. It makes space in your heart where anger once lived. And in that space, love grows.

Contemplation

What am I still carrying that I am ready to release?

What would it feel like to forgive — not for them, but for myself?

Can I begin to see forgiveness as an act of self-love?

Gentle Practice

Take a quiet moment and say these words inwardly — even if you're not ready to fully believe them yet:

"I forgive you.

I release you.

I forgive myself.

I release myself. I choose peace."

Breathe. Allow the healing to begin, even if only a little. You are worthy of freedom.

Chapter 5: Freedom From the Past

The past is not who you are. It is where you've been. It shaped you, yes — but it does not have to define you.

We often live as if our past is a prison. A fixed story. A label we cannot peel off. We carry memories like proof of limitation: "This is who I've always been." "This is what I deserve." "This is what happened, and I can never forget it."

But healing asks us to loosen our grip on that story. Not to deny what happened — but to release the idea that it must follow us forever.

You are not here to endlessly relive your past. You are here to be present, to grow, to evolve.

The truth is, you have changed. In every moment, you are being renewed — not by force, but by willingness. Each breath you take in awareness is a chance to choose again. And the past, no matter how painful, cannot stop you from choosing peace now.

There is a quiet dignity in letting go of old identities. In shedding the masks you wore to survive. In forgiving the version of yourself who didn't yet know what you know today.

Yes, the past taught you. But once the lesson is integrated, you are allowed to move on.

Freedom comes when we stop looking back to decide who we are. Freedom comes when we stop dragging yesterday into today. This moment — this breath — is untainted. Fresh. Sacred. It is a space in which anything is possible, if only we allow ourselves to step into it.

To be free from the past is not to erase your experiences. It is to reclaim your power from them.

You are not broken. You are becoming.

When we stop clinging to the story, we begin to feel the lightness beneath it. We remember that the soul is not bound by time. That love exists outside of memory. That the truest parts of us — the parts made of stillness and light — have never been touched by pain.

This is your invitation: to stop rehearsing your suffering, and start remembering your wholeness.

Freedom is not something you earn. It is something you allow.

Contemplation

What story about myself am I ready to release?

Am I willing to believe that I am more than what has happened to me?

Can I allow today to be different — even if yesterday was painful?

Gentle Practice

Write down one belief you carry from your past that you know is limiting you. Then, on a separate line, write a new truth that empowers you.

For example:

"I am unworthy of love."

→ *"I am learning to love myself more each day."*

Read the new truth aloud. Let it land. Let it live in you.

Part II: LIVING WITH GRACE

Chapter 6: Becoming a Vessel of Light

There is a light within you that is not created by the world — and therefore cannot be taken by the world. It is steady. Eternal. Whole. Even when buried beneath fear, grief, confusion, or doubt, it remains. Untouched. Unbreakable. Waiting to be remembered.

To become a vessel of light is not to become someone new, but to allow more of your true self to shine through. It is not about perfection. It is not about rising above your humanity. It is about learning to live from your center — the part of you that is wise, open, and aligned with love.

A vessel holds. It carries. It pours. In the same way, when you live as a vessel of light, you become a living presence of compassion, calm, and clarity. Not because you are trying to be spiritual, but because you are no longer trying to be anything else.

You allow yourself to be moved by life. You let grace flow through you.

This doesn't mean denying your own needs or always putting others first. In fact, a true vessel must be strong. It must be full. It must be whole. You cannot hold light for the world if you are depleted. Becoming a vessel of light begins with tending to your own inner flame.

Ask yourself: What nourishes my spirit? What helps me return to stillness? What allows me to feel connected, loving, present?

These are not luxuries — they are responsibilities. Because when your inner world is aligned, your outer presence becomes a blessing. You don't have to speak in spiritual words or perform rituals. Your being, your way of listening, your way of walking through the world — it all becomes a silent transmission of light.

And when challenges come, you don't pretend they're not real. You meet them with awareness. You don't collapse. You don't numb. You remember who you are — and let that remembrance guide your response.

This is the quiet power of those who carry light: they do not resist darkness. They transform it.

You don't need to have all the answers. You don't need to be unshakable. All you need is the willingness to be open. To be used by love. To let your presence be a lamp in someone else's night.

Let life pour through you.

Contemplation

What kind of energy do I bring into the spaces I enter?

Am I willing to become a vessel of light — not by doing more, but by being more aligned with love?

What part of me is ready to shine, now that I no longer need to hide?

Gentle Practice

Sit in silence and imagine a gentle light at the center of your chest. Let it grow — not forcefully, but naturally. As you breathe, let it expand to fill your body. Then imagine it radiating beyond you — into your room, your home, your community, your world.

Whisper inwardly:

"May I carry light wherever I go.

May my presence bring peace.

May I remember who I truly am."

Chapter 7: Surrendering to the Flow of Life

Life is not a problem to be solved. It is a river to be trusted.

We spend so much of our energy trying to control — outcomes, people, timing, even ourselves. We tighten our grip in hopes of feeling safe, but all we create is tension. We mistake control for power. But true power is not found in holding on. It is found in letting go.

To surrender is not to give up. It is to give in to the deeper intelligence that lives beneath all things. It is to stop forcing and start flowing. It is to release resistance and allow life to lead — not because we are weak, but because we are wise.

Surrender asks us to loosen our attachment to how things *should* be, so we can meet life as it *is*.

This is not easy for the mind. The mind wants plans, guarantees, and clear destinations. But the soul speaks in softer tones — nudges, intuitions, gentle knowings. It does not shout. It does not rush. It does not demand. It invites.

And when we surrender, we begin to feel that invitation.

We start to notice that not everything is meant to be pushed through. That sometimes, the answer is not effort, but ease. That obstacles may not be blocks, but redirections. That what we thought was failure may actually be protection. That the things we lose may be clearing space for what is truly aligned.

Surrender is not passive. It is profoundly active — because it takes strength to trust.

It takes strength to pause when fear wants you to react. It takes strength to stay open when things don't go as planned. It takes strength to say: *"I don't know what's next, but I trust the unfolding."*

And the more you surrender, the more life begins to feel like a dance — one in which you are no longer trying to lead all the time. You allow life to guide you. You let the current carry you. You stop fighting the river, and you start floating.

The irony is, the more we surrender, the more we return to who we truly are. Because we're no longer chasing some idea of who we think we should be

— we're simply allowing our true nature to emerge.

Let go. Breathe. The river knows the way.

Contemplation

Where am I resisting life right now?

What would it feel like to stop struggling and start trusting?

What might be possible if I allowed life to carry me, instead of trying to control it?

Gentle Practice

Close your eyes and place your palms face up, resting gently on your lap — a physical gesture of openness.

Say silently or aloud:

"I surrender my fear.

I surrender my need to control.

I trust the wisdom of life.

I allow the flow to guide me."

Then take three slow, full breaths — and let the river move through you.

Chapter 8: Living With Humility and Courage

Humility and courage may seem like opposites, but they are, in truth, two wings of the same soul: to live authentically, you must be both grounded and brave. Humility keeps you open, seeing yourself as part of a larger whole.

Courage pushes you to act, even when fear whispers to stay small. Together, they guide you to a life of quiet strength.

Humility is the grace of knowing we are not the center of the universe — and yet, we are intimately connected to all that is. It's the quiet understanding that we don't need to be better than anyone, or have all the answers, to be worthy. Humility softens the ego's edge. It makes space for listening. For learning. For receiving.

Courage is not the absence of fear. It is the willingness to move forward even when fear is present. It is the inner fire that rises when something greater than fear pulls you onward — truth, love, service, integrity.

Together, humility and courage help us walk the path of the heart with steadiness.

Without humility, we close ourselves off from growth. Without courage, we shrink from our potential.

When we live with humility, we don't pretend to know everything. We allow ourselves to be taught — by life, by others, by our own experiences. We release the need to prove ourselves. We become open vessels, able to receive wisdom that can only enter through an unguarded heart.

And when we live with courage, we take responsibility for our presence. We speak the truth when silence would be easier. We act with integrity even when no one is watching. We show up fully — not because it's always comfortable, but because our soul calls us to.

Courage is not loud. It doesn't always roar. Sometimes, courage is simply choosing to get up again. To try again. To love again. To open again — even after being hurt.

And humility? It reminds us that even as we rise, we are still learning. Still unfolding. Still human.

You don't need to have it all figured out to walk in light. You just need the willingness to take the next step — with sincerity, with presence, and with trust.

Humility grounds us. Courage lifts us. Together, they keep us balanced as we navigate both the sacred and the ordinary.

Contemplation

Am I willing to be a student of life — open, curious, and teachable?

Where is life asking me to be braver?

What would humility and courage look like in this moment?

Gentle Practice

Place one hand on your heart and the other over your belly. Breathe deeply. Whisper to yourself:

"I walk with humility.

I rise with courage.

I am willing. I am ready."

Let these words echo softly through your being. Let them guide you forward

— not in perfection, but in presence.

Chapter 9: The Sacred Feminine Within Us All

There is a quiet wisdom that lives in each of us — a soft strength that listens more than it speaks, feels more than it analyzes, holds more than it grasps. This is the sacred feminine. Not as gender, but as essence.

We each carry both feminine and masculine energies within us. The masculine is action, structure, direction. The feminine is intuition, flow, and receptivity. In balance, they harmonize. In imbalance, we feel disconnected — from ourselves, from others, from the deeper rhythm of life.

The sacred feminine is not weak. She is powerful in ways the world often forgets. Her strength is not in force, but in presence. Not in controlling, but in allowing. Not in domination, but in deep, embodied knowing.

When we are disconnected from the sacred feminine, we overvalue doing and undervalue being. We rush. We strive. We override our inner signals in order to meet outer demands. We measure ourselves by productivity, not presence.

But when we return to the feminine within, we remember how to receive. We remember how to feel without shame. We learn to trust the voice inside us that doesn't shout, but simply knows. We move in cycles, not straight lines. We soften — not to collapse, but to become more whole.

The sacred feminine invites us to heal — not by fixing ourselves, but by returning to ourselves.

She invites us to rest, to restore, to connect to the body, to honor intuition, to make space for silence and mystery. She reminds us that life is not only about growth, but also gestation. Not only about expression, but also integration. She honors slowness. She trusts the unseen.

Whether you identify as male, female, neither, or both — the sacred feminine lives within you.

You can feel her in the moments when you are still and fully present. When you cry without resistance. When you sense something without explanation. When you nurture without needing recognition. When you create not for praise, but because it brings you alive.

To awaken the sacred feminine is to return to the wisdom of your inner world. To walk in harmony with your emotions, your cycles, your breath. It is to stop pushing, and start listening.

It is not a rejection of the masculine, but a restoration of balance. A remembering of the wholeness that was always there.

Contemplation

What would it mean for me to honor the sacred feminine within me?

Where in my life am I being called to soften, listen, or receive?

Can I trust the wisdom that arises from my inner knowing?

Gentle Practice

Close your eyes and place both hands gently over your lower belly or heart. Take slow, deep breaths. As you inhale, say inwardly:

"I am open to receive."

As you exhale:

"I trust the wisdom within."

Let yourself be held in the stillness. Let the sacred feminine rise — quietly, powerfully — from within.

Chapter 10: Loving Without Conditions

Most of us have learned to love with conditions.

We offer love when it is safe, when it is earned, when it is returned. We withhold it when we feel rejected, disappointed, or afraid. We call this protection. But often, what we are protecting is not love — it is ego, pride, or an old wound still aching beneath the surface.

True love does not bargain. It does not demand proof. It does not shrink when it is not reciprocated.

True love gives because it is its nature to give.

This kind of love does not mean letting others walk over you. It does not mean accepting abuse or tolerating disrespect. In fact, unconditional love often requires healthy boundaries — not to shut others out, but to keep your own heart clear and clean.

Unconditional love begins with seeing. Really seeing.

Seeing someone not just for what they do, but for who they are beneath their patterns, beneath their pain. It is recognizing the light that still flickers even in the ones who seem furthest from it. And it is remembering that the same light lives in you.

To love without conditions is not to pretend that everything is okay. It is to remain anchored in compassion, even when things are not.

It means loving without needing to fix. Loving without needing to be right.

Loving without needing to win.

It means loving those who trigger us, not by ignoring our emotions, but by choosing to respond from the heart instead of reacting from the wound.

And perhaps most importantly, it means loving yourself in the same way.

Can you love yourself on the days when you fall short?

Can you meet your own flaws with gentleness instead of judgment? Can you stop withholding love from yourself until you "get it right"?

This is where unconditional love begins — not in theory, but in practice. In the ordinary, often difficult moments.

In choosing love again and again, even when it hurts.

Unconditional love is not weak. It is fierce, steady, and quietly revolutionary. It is the force that heals, the energy that transforms, the vibration that lifts the world.

And it lives within you — always waiting to be chosen.

Contemplation

What conditions have I placed on love — for myself or for others?

Can I love even when I do not understand?

What would it feel like to give love without needing anything in return?

Gentle Practice

Close your eyes and take three slow breaths. Place a hand over your heart and say gently:

"I release the need to earn love.

I release the need to control love.

I choose to love — freely, fully, and without fear."

Let that intention echo through you.

Let it shape how you meet the next person, and the next moment.

Part III: EMBODYING THE LIGHT

Chapter 11: Silence, Devotion, and Presence

There is a kind of knowing that cannot be spoken. A kind of love that doesn't need to be declared. A kind of presence that says everything, without saying a word. This is the sacred space where silence, devotion, and presence meet — the quiet, powerful center of the spiritual path.

Silence is more than the absence of sound. It is the inner stillness that allows the soul to breathe.

It is the pause between thoughts, the space between actions, the vastness that holds all things without judgment. In silence, we meet ourselves — not the version shaped by the world, but the truth that has always lived beneath it.

Many fear silence because it reveals. It takes away the distractions we cling to and invites us to feel what we have avoided. But if you stay long enough in silence, you begin to feel held by something deeper — a loving presence that needs no explanation.

Silence is not empty. It is full of truth.

Devotion is the heart's natural posture when it remembers its connection to the sacred. It is not about rituals or rules. It is not reserved for saints or monks.

Devotion is a quality of attention — a loving reverence toward life itself. It is the way you pour tea. The way you breathe before speaking. The way you touch the earth with your feet. The way you return again and again to the quiet source inside you.

Devotion is not loud. It doesn't need to convince or display. It is private, steady, sincere. It is the soul bowing inwardly, saying: *"I am here. I remember."*

Presence is what allows both silence and devotion to become real. Without presence, we sleepwalk through life — distracted, divided, half-alive. But with presence, everything becomes sacred. The ordinary becomes holy. Every interaction, every breath, every moment becomes an opportunity to align with love.

To live with presence is not to escape life — it is to enter it fully. To meet what is here without running.

To listen deeply — to yourself, to others, to the subtle invitations of the soul.

These three — silence, devotion, and presence — do not demand perfection. They ask only your sincerity.

And the more you return to them, the more life begins to feel like a prayer — not made of words, but of awareness.

Contemplation

When was the last time I sat in silence, just to listen?

Where can I bring more devotion into my daily life?

Am I truly present in this moment — or lost in the past or future?

Gentle Practice

Take five minutes today to sit in silence. No agenda. No technique. Simply sit and breathe.

As thoughts come, let them pass like clouds. As you feel distracted, gently return.

Whisper inwardly:

"I am here. This is enough."

Let silence be your teacher. Let presence be your prayer.

Chapter 12: Practices for a Soul-Centered Life

Spiritual awakening is not a goal to reach—it's a way of being, woven through small, intentional choices.

It unfolds slowly, in how we rise each morning, how we speak, how we pause, how we respond, how we choose again and again to live from the center rather than the surface.

A soul-centered life is not perfect. It is not rigid. It is not free from difficulty. It is, however, aligned — guided not by ego, fear, or performance, but by quiet devotion to truth, love, and inner peace.

And while every soul's journey is unique, there are simple, sacred practices that help anchor us in that alignment. Practices that bring us home when we wander. That center us when we forget.

You don't need to do them all. You don't need to do them perfectly. You simply need to return to what resonates — and be sincere.

Here are a few practices to support your path:

1. Begin the Day in Stillness

Before reaching for your phone, before letting the world rush in — take one minute. Sit. Breathe. Place your hand on your heart. Ask:
"How would love have me live today?" "What does my soul need most right now?"
Even one sacred minute can redirect an entire day.

2. Create Rituals, Not Just Routines

Turn the ordinary into something intentional.
Light a candle before journaling. Say a silent prayer while washing your hands. Walk without your phone.
Bless your food.
Ritual slows us down. It returns presence to the present.

3. Practice Conscious Breathing

The breath is your anchor.
When you feel overwhelmed, pause. Inhale slowly…
Exhale even slower.
Let the breath remind you: You are here. You are safe. You are whole.

4. Speak From the Heart

Pause before reacting. Listen before responding.

Ask: Is what I'm about to say necessary? Is it kind? Is it true?

Your words shape energy. Let them be rooted in care.

5. Keep a Sacred Journal

Write not to impress, but to release. To reveal.
Let your journal be a safe space to meet yourself honestly.
Record moments of gratitude, confusion, inspiration, prayer. Over time, your own words will become your mirror and your medicine.

6. Simplify

The soul loves spaciousness.
Let go of what is not essential — in your schedule, your home, your thoughts. Create space for silence, beauty, and rest.
Simplicity is clarity. Clarity is peace.

7. Return to Nature

Walk barefoot. Sit under a tree. Watch clouds move.
Nature is not separate from you — it is your teacher.
Your mirror. Your healing ground.

8. End the Day in Reflection

Before sleep, take a moment to check in.

What moved me today?

Where was I out of alignment — and what can I learn from it? What am I grateful for right now?

Let the day close with awareness — not regret, not judgment, just presence.

These are not rules. They are invitations.

Choose what feels true for you. And know that even small, imperfect steps taken with sincerity are deeply powerful.

A soul-centered life is not a destination. It is a way of walking — with your heart open, your breath steady, and your spirit rooted in the eternal.

Contemplation

Which practices call to me most?

How can I create more space for what nourishes my soul?

Am I willing to make sacred the ordinary?

Gentle Practice

Choose one practice from this chapter. Just one. Do it today — slowly, lovingly, without pressure. Let it be enough. Let it be holy.

Chapter 13: Serving From the Heart

There is a kind of service that uplifts both the giver and the receiver. It does not drain. It does not seek recognition. It arises naturally, quietly, from a place of love.

To serve from the heart is not to lose yourself.

It is to express your truest self in action — to let the light within you touch the world around you.

Many of us were taught that service means sacrifice. That to be good, we must give until we are empty. But true service is not martyrdom. It is not about self-erasure. It is about offering what overflows from within — not because you have to, but because you are moved to.

When service flows from alignment, it nourishes everyone involved.

It doesn't always look like grand gestures. Sometimes it's listening, without trying to fix. Sometimes it's showing up when it's uncomfortable. Sometimes it's the way you tend to a child, a plant, a stranger, a friend — with full attention and an open heart.

Your presence is your greatest gift.

Not your perfection. Not your performance.

But the way you show up — sincerely, gently, humbly.

Service becomes sacred when it is rooted in love, not obligation. When it is guided by inner truth, not outer approval.

When it is offered with reverence, not resentment.

To serve from the heart is to remember that your life is not separate from the whole. That your healing, your joy, your growth — all ripple outward. You don't have to try to change the world. You only need to be in alignment with your soul. That alone changes everything.

And when you serve with love, life supports you. You are not left behind. You are not forgotten.

The energy you give, when pure, returns to you — not always in the way you expect, but always in the way you need.

You don't have to do it all.

You only have to do your part — with presence, with care, with heart.

Contemplation

What am I here to give — not for approval, but from authenticity?

What does service mean to me, when stripped of guilt or pressure?

Can I offer something today — even something small — from a place of love?

Gentle Practice

Offer a quiet act of service today.

It can be simple: a kind word, a helping hand, a silent prayer, a generous pause.

Don't announce it. Don't track it. Just give.

Let your heart be the reason. Let love be the reward.

Chapter 14: Transforming Suffering Into Strength

Pain is a part of being human. It visits all of us —
through loss, betrayal, illness, heartbreak, fear. We
cannot escape it. But we can transform it.

There is a difference between pain and suffering.

Pain is an experience. Suffering is the story we wrap
around that experience. It is the resistance, the clinging,
the belief that things should be different. It is not the
wound itself, but our refusal to let the wound heal.

The path of the soul is not about avoiding suffering. It is
about learning to meet pain with presence — and allow it
to become a doorway to something deeper.

Every scar carries a story. Every ache is a teacher. And
while we may not choose our suffering, we can choose
what we do with it.

We can choose to let it open us instead of close us. To let
it deepen us instead of harden us.

To let it reveal our strength, our tenderness, our capacity
to rise.

Transformation begins when we stop asking, *"Why me?"*

and start asking,

"What now?"

What am I being shown?

What within me is ready to be opened?

What is this pain inviting me to release, to learn, to become?

When we turn toward our suffering — instead of running or numbing — we begin to discover something remarkable: we are not as fragile as we feared. The very places we thought would break us are often where the light enters.

This doesn't mean romanticizing pain. It means honoring it. Being honest about it. And allowing it to alchemize you from within.

Your suffering is not your identity. It is your initiation.

Let it refine you, not define you. Let it soften you, not shatter you.

Let it teach you compassion — for yourself, and for every soul who has ever silently carried their own heavy grief.

There is wisdom on the other side of pain.

There is peace that comes not from avoiding storms, but from learning to stand in the center of them — steady, open, awake.

You are not being punished. You are being reshaped.

Contemplation

What pain am I still holding — and how have I resisted it?

What strength has emerged from my darkest moments?

Am I willing to let this pain teach me, rather than define me?

Gentle Practice

Take a moment to place your hands gently over your heart. Breathe into the space of tenderness.

Whisper inwardly:

"I honor my pain.

I do not resist it.

I allow it to transform me.

I am becoming stronger, softer, and more whole."

Let your breath move through the places that ache. You are not broken. You are becoming.

Chapter 15: The Way of the Light Within

At the heart of your being, beyond all the layers of identity, effort, and history, there is a light.

It is not something you must earn. It is not something you must search for. It is who you already are.

This light is your essence — steady, clear, loving, and aware.

It is untouched by fear, untouched by failure, untouched by the passing storms of life.

You may forget it. You may lose sight of it.

But it never leaves you. It only waits to be remembered.

To live from the light within is not to escape the world.

It is to move through the world with deep presence and quiet strength.

It is to let your actions be guided not by fear or approval, but by your inner knowing — the soft voice that always points you toward love, integrity, and truth.

The way of the light is not loud. It doesn't force. It doesn't push.

It invites. It illuminates. It simply is.

When you live from this light, you don't become someone else. You become more fully yourself.

You no longer try to prove or impress.

You no longer seek love — you become it.

You no longer need to chase peace — you carry it.

This doesn't mean life becomes easy. It means you become anchored.

Rooted in what is real. Aligned with what is sacred. Awake in the midst of the ordinary.

Living from the light within is a choice — a daily, moment-by-moment practice.

It is choosing compassion over judgment. Presence over distraction.

Trust over control. Stillness over noise. Love over fear.

And when you forget — as we all do — you return. Gently. Quietly. Without shame.

You place your hand over your heart. You breathe.

And you remember:

The light was never gone. I simply closed my eyes.

And now, I open them again.

Contemplation

What does it mean, to live from my light?

What habits or beliefs dim that light — and am I ready to release them?

How would I walk, speak, love, and serve if I fully trusted the light within me?

Gentle Practice

Sit quietly. Let your body soften. Let your breath be gentle.

Imagine a light glowing in your heart — soft, warm, radiant. Let it expand, gently, until you feel it in every part of you.

Repeat inwardly:

"I am light.

I carry love.

I walk in peace.

I remember who I am."

Let this be the beginning, not the end — a return to yourself, and a life lived from the inside out.

Part IV: WALKING WITH THE LIGHT WITHIN — A COMPANION GUIDE FOR DAILY REFLECTION

An Invitation Inward

This is not a program to complete, nor a task to check off. This is a gentle invitation to pause. To listen. To soften into what is already here.

Each page that follows is a doorway—quietly opening you to a deeper way of being.
You are not asked to change yourself. You are simply invited to remember yourself.

Let the days unfold as slowly as needed. Read one a day, or whenever your heart asks for a moment of stillness.

There is no rush. No requirement. Only a return.

Let this be a soft beginning.

Day 1 — Begin Again

Where in your life are you being invited to begin again?

Even in moments of doubt, stillness, or regret, life gently opens its hands and whispers: *Start here. Start now.*

To begin again is not weakness. It is strength wrapped in grace.

Quiet Practice

Sit in silence for a few minutes. As you breathe, repeat softly within:
I begin again. This moment is new.

Invitation for Reflection

What does "beginning again" mean to you right now?

Day 2 — Let It Be Simple

Peace is rarely found in the complexity we chase.
It lives quietly in the ordinary. In the breath. In the now.

Simplicity is not the absence of meaning—it is the return
to it.

Quiet Practice

Choose one task today—washing a cup, folding clothes,
stepping outside. Let it become your meditation. Nothing
more is needed.

Invitation for Reflection

Where can I simplify today—both around me and within
me?

Day 3 — Trust the Flow

What if the moment doesn't need fixing? What if life is already moving, even when I don't understand the direction?

Control is exhausting. Trust is soft. It lets the current carry what I cannot.

Quiet Practice

Rest your palms open on your lap. Breathe gently. Whisper inwardly:
I release. I allow. I trust.

Invitation for Reflection

Where am I holding on too tightly?
What might open if I trusted the flow?

Day 4 — Sit With Yourself

You are not a project. Not a puzzle to solve.
You are a presence to sit beside, lovingly and without judgment.

Stillness isn't empty. It's a return.

Quiet Practice

Sit for a few minutes with no agenda. Feel your breath.
Let your thoughts pass. Stay present with whatever arises.

Invitation for Reflection

What am I feeling today—beneath the noise, beneath the roles?

Day 5 — Offer Compassion

Compassion is not always grand or visible.
Sometimes it looks like staying. Listening. Breathing with.

You do not need the perfect words. Your presence is enough.

Quiet Practice

Close your eyes and silently send this blessing to yourself or another:
May you be safe. May you be free. May you know you are loved.

Invitation for Reflection

Where is compassion needed today?
Can I begin by offering it to myself?

Day 6 — Stay With What's Real

Thoughts race. Emotions swirl. But beneath them is the truth of the moment: the breath, the heartbeat, the presence of being here.

Reality is not always easy, but it is always sacred.

Quiet Practice

Pause often today. Touch the ground with your feet or hand. Whisper inwardly:
This is what's real.

Invitation for Reflection

What do I notice in my breath, my body, or my heart right now?

Day 7 — Walk in Light

You are not searching for light.
You are remembering it.

You were never meant to earn your worth. You were
meant to embody it.

Quiet Practice

Place a hand on your heart. Breathe deeply and say:
I remember. I return. I walk in light.

Invitation for Reflection

What would it mean to walk in light today—not for
anyone else, but for myself?

Part V: CLOSING REFLECTIONS

A Letter to the One Who Feels Lost

Dear one,

If you're holding this book and feeling uncertain, know this: you are not alone. There are moments in life when the light feels dim, and the path ahead seems hidden in fog. But even in the quiet ache of confusion or pain, the light within you still flickers—gentle, steady, waiting.

You do not need to know the answers. You do not need to rush. You are not behind. You are not broken. You are simply here.

Let each breath bring you closer to yourself. Let these words be a soft place to land.

In your own time, in your own way—you will find your way forward.

With care,
Fuchen

Living the Light

I did not write this book from a mountaintop of certainty. I wrote it while walking through my own valleys—pausing, listening, returning. The words came in whispers, in the still moments between striving.

"The Light Within" is not a teaching as much as it is a remembering. I return to these truths myself, again and again. Stillness is not something I master. It is something I meet—daily, imperfectly, with grace.

If these pages have offered you even a sliver of peace or clarity, I am grateful. Let us keep walking, gently, toward what matters most.

Three Quiet Reminders

1. You are not behind.

Life unfolds on no one's schedule but your soul's.
Breathe. Trust your rhythm. You are exactly where you
are meant to be.

2. Stillness is always available.

No matter how loud the world becomes, you can return to
your breath, your body, your being. Even one quiet
moment can shift everything.

3. You are already whole.

Nothing needs fixing for you to be enough. Your worth is
not earned—it is remembered.

Let these truths anchor you.

Closing Blessing: A Final Offering from the Heart

The journey doesn't end here. It continues wherever you are willing to pause, soften, and return.

If these words have touched something in you — not just in your mind, but in your soul — then the light within you is already awakening.

Carry these words lightly. Let them settle into your days like quiet rain nourishing the roots of your own becoming.

There is nothing more to prove. You are already enough.

This book was never meant to give you something you didn't already have. It was meant to remind you of what was always there.

The path of love, presence, and inner truth is not far away.

It begins here — with your next breath, your next choice, your next moment of awareness.

You don't need to become someone else.

You don't need to chase a better version of yourself.

You only need to return — again and again — to what is already whole within you.

Even when you forget, you can return. Even when you fall, you can rise.

Even in your most human moments, you are still sacred.

So may you walk forward with softness and strength. May you meet yourself and the world with gentleness.

May you find peace in the silence, and light in the shadows. May you trust the wisdom that lives in your heart.

And above all — may you remember:

You are not lost. You are not broken.

You are already home.

Thank you for walking this journey. May the light within you shine freely, and may you become a blessing wherever you go.

With gratitude,
Fuchen

About the Author

Fuchen Yew was educated and trained as an electrical engineer in the United States and worked in the North American telecommunications industry before returning to his home country of Malaysia in 2005. There, a series of encounters with spiritual teachers opened the doorway to a lifelong path of inner transformation.

Over the past two decades, Fuchen has immersed himself in spiritual learning, contemplation, and soul-centered living. His writing reflects a quiet devotion to truth, presence, and love — offered in a universal language that speaks to the heart, regardless of belief or background.

He lives in Malaysia with his family, continuing his inner practice and sharing reflections with those seeking a more peaceful, grounded, and awakened life.

The Light Within:
An Invitation to Inner Stillness and Grace

In "*The Light Within*," Fuchen Yew invites readers on a transformative journey to rediscover the inner stillness and grace that resides in each of us. Through personal reflections and gentle practices, he encourages a deep connection with the present moment, fostering healing, authenticity, and the sacredness of service. This book serves as a heartfelt reminder that the light we seek is already within, waiting to illuminate our path home.

www.ingramcontent.com/pod-product-compliance
Lightning Source LLC
LaVergne TN
LVHW051154080426
835508LV00021B/2623